I0109826

Fearless Leadership

How High-Performing Organizations Are Transforming the Workplace!

Copyright © 2012 Yagos & Associates

ISBN 10: 098485304
ISBN 13: 978-0-9848538-0-9

All rights reserved. No part of this publication may be reproduced, stored in a retrieval system, or transmitted in any form or by any means, electronic, mechanical, recording or otherwise, without the prior written permission of the author.

Printed in the United States of America.

The author of this book is offering information of a general nature for educational purposes. If you use any information in this book for yourself, the author and publisher assume no responsibility for your actions and cannot be held liable in any way for the results of financial, business, or personal decisions made based upon the information contained herein. The author and publisher also cannot be held responsible for any errors or omissions in this book.

Thomas J. Yagos

www.YagosAssociates.com

Fearless Leadership

How High-Performing Organizations Are Transforming the Workplace!

Thomas J. Yagos

Dedication

This book is dedicated to Gladys Moore

(1922 –1992)

You have changed my life forever.

Contents

Acknowledgments

In 1985, I met a woman who would change my life forever. Gladys Moore was a delightful person who loved life. Her eyes sparkled, her smile radiated with excitement, and her voice filled with passion when she talked about how we can live our lives with love and joy. Before Gladys died in 1992, she shared her knowledge and the keys for how to experience personal and professional relationships based on acceptance, enjoyment, and trust.

Many of the concepts I will convey to you are from Gladys Moore's teachings, experiences, stories, and insights on how to use our mind correctly, free of fear. I share the concepts knowing it takes courage, practice, patience, and forgiveness to use them each day to change our lives. It takes self-belief and a desire to experience a new way of thinking—using the mind to experience more enjoyment. It requires being aware of when fear is present in our responses and identifying what we can do to make the changes.

I invite you to use these concepts to improve the relationships you experience each day. This book is a guide for anyone that is interested in improving their relationships, both personally and professionally. You can do it if you choose to take the steps. Don't let the fear of feeling rejected or inadequate control your life as it once did mine. The focus of this book is on the workplace, where employees at every level spend countless hours each day in community with others.

I am grateful to the senior executives that have encouraged me to share the concepts in the workplace to eliminate the legacy of fear. I also am deeply appreciative of over 1000 students who attended my leadership class and were courageous in sharing their insights about fear in the workplace. I want to thank my friends, Carol Messmer, Sally Ogden, Jere Hart, Linda Macey, and Howard Hoffer, wherever your energy may be. Special appreciation goes to my spouse Kathy (who introduced me to Gladys Moore), for her support and encouragement in writing this book.

Your journey awaits you—to experience your life in a state of love and joy!

Thomas J. Yagos

Introduction

My Calling for Writing this Book

I have read countless books and articles, listened to numerous speakers and audiotapes, and attended a plethora of workshops and educational programs designed with learning initiatives on leadership, team building, stress management, succession planning, process improvement, strategic planning, quality control, and performance improvement. Yet, in my 35 years of senior leadership experience, consulting, and teaching at a university, the topic of "fear in the workplace" has not been addressed by most organizations. My belief is that organizations must put this topic on the table and provide solutions to displace fear and build trust. We can continue to design new training initiatives and engage more leadership consultants, but until we deal with fear, organizations will continue to struggle with employee engagement and organizational effectiveness.

Employees are the ambassadors of an organization, and the success of the organization should be built on a foundation of inspired and engaged employees. Based on my 13 years of research and over 1000 interviews, 64% of employees interviewed (of which 40% were managers) believe that fear is present to some degree in all organizations today. You may wonder, what type of fear? It's the fear of change, failure, taking a risk, falling revenue, speaking up, or the news of a potential layoff.

Fear in the workplace causes fear-based behaviors, which paralyze employees and lead to mistrust throughout the organization. I believe the underlying factor of fear needs to be managed, reduced, and eliminated before employee engagement can be sustained at all levels that impact organizational effectiveness.

This book is designed not to engage confrontation with those who believe that fear motivates employees, but to provide a different perspective on how to inspire employees to reach a new level of trust without using fear.

Fear Can Permeate the Structure of an Organization

If left unchecked, fear permeates the relationships, structures, processes, policies, and management styles of an organization, creating a culture of fear. A fear-based culture depletes pride, undermines quality, reduces profitability, and stifles productivity. Fear impacts how we use our interpersonal skills to communicate, make decisions, inspire others, build teams, and resolve conflicts, to the detriment of the organization.

A traditional organization may have a board of directors that is responsible for representing the stakeholders. The board is also responsible for working with the Chief Executive Officer (CEO) to formulate the strategy for the organization. The CEO provides guidance and works with the executive team to align the processes, systems, resources, and employees to implement the goals and objectives. These goals and objectives are shared with the executives' direct reports, who communicate them throughout the rest of the organization.

The goals and objectives provide direction for all the employees, and a powerful culture can be created in the organization when employee behaviors are aligned with the strategy. These behaviors can build relationships based on a foundation of trust when employees feel respected, valued, and receive consideration—or these relationships can be built on fear when employees feel abused and treated unfairly.

If the board of directors creates fear in the CEO and the executive team with threats of dismissal, loss of promotions, reduction in compensation, or for a variety of other reasons, this fear of the unknown, change, and failure can cascade downward throughout the organization. If not managed, reduced, or eliminated, the fear is operationalized into the day-to-day activities of the organization. It affects the executive team and its direct reports, and then filters down to the managers, supervisors, and finally, the employees that are performing the tasks.

I worked with a CEO of a financial services company who, in front of his senior staff and their direct reports, threatened to dismiss the entire business development team if he didn't see sales improve in the next 90 days—and then he left the room. How do you think the business development team felt when they heard the news? What were their behaviors like? I can tell you, they felt defeated and depressed. His announcement had a negative impact on all the employees, and fear ran rampant throughout the organization.

When fear is introduced at the senior level and cascades down through the executive team, director, and vice-president levels, and then to the manager and supervisor levels, fear-based behaviors become the norm to survive. This culture of fear may take years to change.

Conditions that Promote Fear

Figure 1 shows conditions that promote fear, impact performance, and carry a high cost to the organization.

Conditions that Promote Fear	Impact on Performance	Costs to the Organization
•Micromanagement	•Overtime	•Objectives neglected
•Hidden agendas	•Poor communication	•Wasted resources
•Unethical behaviors	•Self-serving interest	•Delayed projects
•Stress	•Poor quality of work	•Healthcare
•Redundant systems	•Heavy workload	•Retraining
•Lack of trust	•Absence of innovation	•Turnover / absenteeism
•Bureaucracy	•Delays in service	•Policies / procedures
•Grievances	•Labor unrest	•Lawsuits
•Missed deadlines	•Complaints	•Lost customers

Figure 1 – Conditions that Promote Fear

A potential solution to reduce these costs is to reduce fear. When we reduce and manage fear in the workplace, employees enjoy coming to work with renewed passion. Absenteeism and turnover decrease, and morale improves. Employees become more inspired in the work they do. Productivity increases, which benefits the customers, employees, and company. Does this sound too simple, too idealistic? Franklin D. Roosevelt said, "The only thing we have to fear is fear itself." I wonder if we truly understand the implications of this quote and comprehend what fear has done to the workplace.

According to W. Edwards Deming, "Many employees are afraid to ask questions or take a position, even when they don't understand what their job is or what is right or wrong. The economic losses from fear are appalling." Deming further states, "The job of the leader is to understand that the system is composed of people." To minimize and manage fear, leaders must create an environment where employees can share information without concern about repercussions. (Deming, 1990).

Measuring the true cost of fear is not an exact science. It doesn't have a line item in a financial statement; yet leaders intuitively know there is a cost, which reveals itself in employee behaviors of anger, frustration, tension, and anxiety.

During this time of uncertainty in the world, business leaders recognize that the workplace is changing. They are interested in improving relationships in the workplace; and employees are demanding changes. They want a voice in the work they do and how they are treated. The success of the company depends upon solutions for building trusting relationships. According to an article, *The Decision to Trust,* authored by Robert F. Hurley and published in 2006 in the Harvard Business Review, 450 executives from 30 companies were interviewed, and over 50% did not trust their leaders. I believe the culture of fear is a significant underlying contributor to this statistic.

To make the workplace a healthier environment, we must manage the culture of fear. When we reduce and manage fear, we can reinstate the foundation of trust, using our interpersonal skills differently and building trusting relationships.

Releasing fear, asking for peace of mind, and changing one's thought process is a new approach to improving relationships. The awareness of fear and the damage it can cause to an organization should provide the initiative to make changes. It is not a quick-fix process, as it took time to create such conditions in the workplace. The fears of rejection and inadequacy reveal themselves through people's behavior, creating a barrier to well-functioning teams and organizations. Fear-based behaviors not only are self-defeating, they bring about the untold economic losses Deming refers to. If left unchecked, fear can lead to the demise of an organization.

Research by Towers and Perrin points out, year after year, that the U.S. workforce remains a place where less than one-third of the employees truly can be described as "engaged." In addition, the study reveals that hundreds of billions of dollars are lost in the U.S. economy each year. (Towers and Perrin, 2008)

What is a potential solution? For employee engagement to increase and remain high, a fundamental shift must take place. An organization needs a solid culture and value system that supports the elements necessary for engagement. Managing, reducing and eliminating fear to build trust helps increase the level of employee engagement in the workplace.

The Future Workplace

Employees want to work in an environment that gives their lives meaning. They seek organizations whose vision and values are aligned with their own. They want a values-enriched culture that encourages creativity and innovation. Such a culture demands an evolved leadership approach of building relationships on a foundation of trust—a foundation that can be built only when fear is reduced and managed in the workplace.

Unfortunately, there is little guidance in management training courses to help leaders deal with fear in the workplace. Fear can never truly be eliminated; however, we can take steps to manage and reduce it in the workplace. This book is structured to help leaders and organizations worldwide to understand where fear comes from, and how to manage and reduce fear in order to build trust in the workplace.

My goal is to facilitate making the workplace a trusting environment not only for this generation, but for future generations that will take on leadership roles. By taking this journey with me, you will discover what a workplace can be like when fear is not part of the culture. More importantly, I will share the concepts and tools that may change your life—both personally and professionally—forever. I hope this book inspires you so that you may inspire others to change.

Fearless Leadership is a resource for every person in every workplace who wants to experience relationships based on acceptance, enjoyment, and trust. More importantly, it provides the knowledge, skills, and tools for how to accomplish this, creating a framework for raising the level of employee engagement in the workplace.

Everyone has a journey in this life and a destiny to awaken the knowing that resides in each of us.
I would like to share my purpose, destiny, cause, and calling with you.

Purpose in My Being

Experience the journey of life in a state of love and joy.

Destiny

Create a loving and caring environment where relationships are experienced with acceptance, enjoyment, and love.

Cause

Personal: Inspire everyone in all communities to live their lives with love by transcending fear and becoming a light for others to follow.

Workplace: Ignite the spirit of individuals in organizations to reawaken their values, to where work is spiritually fulfilling and nurtures the soul of each individual.

Calling

Teaching, writing, facilitating, speaking, and volunteering to promote a caring community, exploring new ideas by being a lifelong learner.

Personal Commitment

Before you begin this book, I request your courageous commitment to:

➢ Explore your purpose, destiny, cause, and calling for being on this earth. How will you live your life?

➢ Use this book to journal your thoughts, ideas, experiences, "ah-ha" moments, and personal reflections. Keep it with you, and reflect at the end of the day with three questions:

- Did I build trust or create fear in the lives I touched today?

- What will I do differently tomorrow?

- How will I inspire others?

Thomas J. Yagos

Chapter 1

Workplace Vignettes

~ ~ ~

Fear is the psychological, emotional, and spiritual opposite of love. No one is inspired by fear. People may be motivated by fear, but never inspired by it.
–Lance Secretan

The first step on this journey is to examine several workplace vignettes to compare and contrast the characteristics of managers and workplaces that are with and without fear, observing how they use their interpersonal skills differently. Today, organizations exist on a continuum between fear and trust. Some are focused on building high trust and performance with their employees, while others are holding onto the past paradigm of command and control that leads to fear and mistrust.

Vignettes and Observations

To illustrate how fear may permeate an organization, let's explore several vignettes that might occur in an organization. These examples are taken from true stories shared by employees I have coached over the years.

Senior Executive, Closed-Door Meetings

Brian, the Chief Financial Officer (CFO) of a manufacturing company, walked by his CEO's office and noticed that David, the CEO, was meeting with Brian's direct reports. David saw the CFO, yet did not invite him into the meeting. The team was working on the installation of a financial reporting system. The implementation was behind schedule, but Brian had assured the executive team that deadlines would be met.

Brian began to speculate about what was going on with his team and why David didn't ask him to join the meeting. He knew the system installation had some challenges. His mind played through various scenarios, and he wondered what they were discussing. Was David disappointed—might he be considering having someone else head the project? Surely, that was not possible! Brian began to question more, as his mind searched for possible explanations. He became angry at his reports for not telling him about the meeting, and considered taking punitive action because they had bypassed him. It was past 6:30 p.m., and the team still was in the meeting with the CEO. As Brian drove home, preoccupied with the day's events, he was physically upset and felt knots in his stomach.

What was driving Brian's behavior at work and on the way home? What might Brian's behavior be like the next day, and what might be the impact on his performance?

_____

_____

_____

_____

_____

Healthcare Manager in a Downward Spiral

Julianne, the director of Radiology, had just finished debriefing her team about patient schedules when a senior physician interrupted the meeting. The physician chastised Julianne for the slow response to his patients. For the next few minutes, he continued to belittle her performance and service capabilities in front of her staff without allowing her a word to clarify her position and discuss his expectations. Her staff walked away as the physician continued to berate her. She looked at the physician and yelled, "That's enough—I have had it with your demeaning behavior! Don't ever talk to me again." Julianne went into her office, closed the blinds, canceled her meetings for the rest of the day, and started to cry. She questioned whether she wanted to continue to work at that hospital, as she did not feel appreciated. At that moment, she vowed to look for another position.

What is Julianne experiencing during the conversation with the physician and when she goes back to her office? What impact might Julianne's behavior have on the team's performance for the rest of the day?

_____

_____

_____

_____

_____

_____

Lack of Feedback—Poor Performance

Jonathan was transferred to the Purchasing department as part of a management development program, filling a role on the Purchasing team that supported requests from production plants. Janet, his manager, assigned Marianne to mentor him for the next 90 days as he learned about the department. Jonathan was given several projects to work on independently;

Marianne occasionally asked him for an update. He noticed that Marianne and Janet reviewed his work, yet provided very little feedback.

Marianne had asked that Jonathan check with her on all requests from the various plants. When Jonathan queried Janet (whom he saw infrequently) and Marianne regarding his performance in the department, both of them responded with, "Fine." Jonathan started to worry about his performance, since he wasn't receiving feedback. He wondered if he still would be part of the management program. His performance started to decline; he was slow to respond to requests from the field and made excuses for not attending staff meetings. Finally, Jonathan walked into Janet's office, closed the door, and demanded an explanation for what was going on in the department. He was blunt, accusatory, and obviously frustrated about the lack of feedback he had experienced in the past 60 days.

What is driving Jonathan's behavior in the workplace? What impact has it had on his performance?

_____

_____

_____

_____

Micromanagers at Their Best—High Alert

Jacqueline, a senior vice president, micromanaged her direct reports even though they were very talented in their roles. She did not feel secure unless she was personally involved with the details of their activities. Her inability to delegate had little to do with her reports, but was due to her choice of doubt over trust. She viewed the slightest mistake as a threat to her reputation.

What is Jacqueline experiencing in the workplace? What impact could her performance have on the rest of her team?

_____

_____

_____

_____

_____

_____

Kristine's Story: The Team Is Dysfunctional

Kristine, the chief strategy officer for a public utility company, was responsible for assembling individual business plans and reports from the executive team. Many of the team members did not have their plans completed on a timely basis, as requested by the CEO. Kristine was concerned about her relationship with her colleagues as well as with the CEO, whom she reported to. In an effort to cover for her colleagues, she avoided several requests from the CEO's assistant to meet with the CEO.

What is driving Kristine's behavior in the workplace?

_____

_____

_____

_____

_____

_____

_____

Truth-Telling in the Workplace

Vaughan, a project manager, was in charge of a project that was six weeks behind schedule and over budget. Everyone on the team knew the project was in trouble, but in presenting a status report to the customer, Vaughan said everything was fine. His inaccurate report led the people who depended on the project to believe it would be done on time. Work piled up, deadlines were missed, and clients were disappointed—all because the project manager didn't feel safe in telling the truth in the workplace.

What is Vaughan experiencing? What is the impact of his behavior on the rest of the team?

_____

_____

_____

_____

_____

_____

Can You Relate to Any of These Workplace Vignettes?

What did you observe about these workplace vignettes? What inferences can you make about the workplaces?

_____

_____

_____

_____

_____

_____

What did you observe about the behaviors of these employees?

_____

_____

_____

_____

_____

_____

There aren't any right or wrong answers; these are your personal insights from reading the vignettes. If your thoughts focused on several of these individuals feeling *rejected or inadequate* and responding with a fear-based behavior, you agree with me in your thinking and understanding.

With this information in mind, let's examine the characteristics of a workplace where managers use fear to motivate employees. These characteristics create a culture of mistrust where no one is inspired to work at their best. When managers create fear in their employees (either intentionally or unintentionally), there are consequences and characteristics that emerge in these workplaces. Figure 2 shows the continuum of feelings that range from fear to trust.

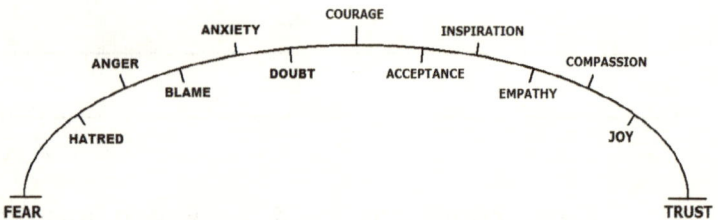

Figure 2 – Fear-Trust Continuum

Over the years, I have worked for and with organizations that exhibit "fear-culture" characteristics, to the detriment of the employees and the organization. These characteristics, if left unchecked, can become a cancer to the organization.

Characteristics of a Workplace with Fear

Employees in a Fear-Culture Workplace

Employees in fear-culture workplaces tend to exhibit the following characteristics. These employees:

- Do just enough to get by, making no extra effort.
- Complain to each other after meetings.
- Are offered very little training.
- Are subject to unrealistic deadlines.
- Resist performance reviews.
- File complaints and grievances.

- Have high absenteeism and often are late to meetings.
- Feel constantly stressed because there are too many projects.
- Experience loss of credibility and diminished opportunity for advancement.
- Waste resources and lack concern for quality.
- Take credit for other people's work.
- Want to transfer to other departments.
- Lose self-esteem due to demotions.
- Have frequent turnover in positions.
- Lack pride in the work they perform.

Managers in a Fear-Culture Workplace

Managers in fear-culture organizations also exhibit certain characteristics that support the climate of fear and mistrust. When managers express these characteristics, it sends a message to the employees that they are not respected and valued.

Characteristics of a manager in a fear-culture workplace include:

- Doesn't want to hear difficult or bad news.

- Continuously bullies employees.

- Retaliates against those who make mistakes.

- Behaves unethically, cuts corners, and uses inaccurate reporting.

- Yells and swears in order to intimidate employees.

- Publicly criticizes employees with insults and putdowns.

- Sets unrealistic timelines so that employees work longer hours.

- Uses favoritism to reward loyal employees.

- Lacks concern for employees' personal issues and family matters.

- Abuses power by blaming and discrediting employees and their work.

- Makes all the decisions because he or she doesn't trust others.

- Starts rumors to motivate employees to work harder.
- Micromanages employees' work to ensure it is completed in his or her way.

From this description, can you identify managers you've had? How do employees use their interpersonal skills in a fear-based environment? Remember that how we use our skills comes from our learned behavior, and our behavior is shaped by our personality. We are on "automatic pilot" most of the time. To change our behavior requires awareness and an acknowledgement of how we are currently behaving. It may be helpful to reflect on the following questions:

- How do employees communicate with each other?
- How are decisions made?
- How is conflict resolved?
- How are employees inspired?
- How do employees embrace change?
- How do employees participate on teams?

How Does This Impact an Organization's Performance?

When we work with this type of manager, a culture of fear often is created. We use our interpersonal skills differently; our communication tends to be guarded rather than open and honest, and conflicts with colleagues are approached with a "win-lose" mindset because the manager makes all the decisions. In this environment, the employees undermine change by working around the initiatives, which leads to poor results. Teams are dysfunctional, with individuals focused on themselves rather than on the team. Panic sets in and rumors circulate as deadlines are missed, leading to poor performance and lost customers. Employees are motivated to keep their heads down and stay out of the manager's way. Innovation and creativity are stifled because risk-taking is not allowed. No one is inspired to work in this type of environment or for this type of manager.

Managers who employ fear tactics use them for personal gain, not to accomplish organizational objectives. "When employees feel disconnected from the organization, they behave in counterproductive ways. They work in silos and survival behaviors become the norm." (Malandro, 2009)

Leaders Are Responsible for Initiating Efforts to Reduce Fear and Build Trust

Let's explore Maslow's Hierarchy of Needs, the pyramid with five levels (Figure 3). The first level satisfies physiological needs (air, water, food, shelter, warmth, sex, and sleep), the second level satisfies security needs (working in a safe, stable, and secure environment), and the third level identifies social needs (belonging, affection, and family). The fourth level is self-esteem (recognition and status), and the fifth level is self-actualization (personal growth).

Figure 3 – Maslow's Hierarchy of Needs

You move from level to level as your needs are satisfied and you experience trust. However, when we introduce the "psychological fear" of feeling rejected or inadequate in the workplace, which threatens employees' security, they may fall several levels to focus on safety and security needs, wondering, "Do I have a job?" Many of these employees may find it difficult to move back up to the previous levels of self-esteem and self–actualization, where personal growth takes place, benefiting the employee and the organization.

A culture of fear plays a significant role in the loss of productivity, profitability, quality, and customers. It increases stress and turnover in the staff. Reflect on these questions for a moment: Can you identify the characteristics of a workplace with fear? Are you able to identify the traits of managers who lead with fear, and see how they use their skills in this environment to create a culture of fear?

Many employees have worked in this type of environment, as have I. Employees who remain in a fear-based environment tend to be less productive, lack creativity, resist change, and often lack accountability and undermine authority. Fear, like other negative reinforcements, can never produce the desired level of performance. Employees that are preoccupied by fear are likely to be engaged in survival behaviors that serve to protect them. How would you be inspired—and what would be your level of engagement—in a workplace controlled by fear?

"The fundamental problem in American business is that people are scared to discuss the problems of people." (Giltow and Giltow, 1987) Fear is indeed a problem of people. It does exist in the workplace and works its destruction because we refuse to face it.

"Fear is a force that robs employees and organizations of their potential." (Ryan and Osterich, 1998). To build trust and eliminate fear, business leaders must be willing to make changes in their personal style. The key is *self-awareness*. Talking about fear and observing the signs of fear in the workplace are major steps toward acknowledeging that it exists.

The research fndings I have collated from more than 1000 participants over the past

13 years reveal that an average of 64% dislike their tasks, their manager, and the organization. Over 45% of the participants were in management roles. They felt the ingredient of *fear* was an underlying contributor to their feelings about their tasks, managers, and organization. Once we understand fear, we can start the process of managing, reducing, and eliminating it.

Fear may motivate employees in the short term, but in the long term it can destroy an organization. Many senior executives believe a " dose of fear" is healthy, but *how much is the dose before it damages the organization?* Fear creates stress in employees, and is of no benefit or value. Why take the risk? It destroys trust and can be terminal to the organization. Figure 4 provides a humorous example of the pervasiveness of the use of fear as a motivator.

Figure 4 – Cheer or Fear?

Figure 5 illustrates how rapidly—and insidiously—fear can spread among people.

Ed Stein, reprinted with permission

Figure 5 – The Contagion of Fear

Characteristics of a Fear-Free Workplace

A fear-free workplace promotes enjoyable relationships. Let's examine the characteristics of a workplace without fear-based behaviors.

In a workplace free of fear, employees:

- Feel inspired and passionate about their work.
- Are respectful and considerate of each other.
- Are willing to help one another and exchange information.
- Enjoy coming to work, and experience the workplace as safe and secure.
- Are knowledgeable and feel valued for their work.
- Speak up with new ideas and are open to change.
- Experience humor, fun, and enjoyment as part of the culture.
- Take responsibility for their choices.

- Govern themselves.
- Place more importance on team performance than on individual achievement.
- Are encouraged to be creative and innovative.
- Have a high level of ethics and respect for diversity.

When you are free of fear,
a whole new world opens up.

Characteristics of a Manager in a Fear-Free Workplace

Managers that build trust express a passion and enthusiasm for learning and developing their employees. They have the courage to speak to their peers and managers about the negative impact of fear in the workplace.

A manager in a fear-free workplace:

- Respects employees and takes time to listen to their concerns.

- Is inspired and inspires others.
- Offers timely feedback without criticism.
- Matches employees' skills to the tasks.
- Recognizes individual contributions, both privately and publicly.
- Encourages everyone's participation at meetings.
- Is open to change and suggestions for improvement.
- Promotes a work-life balance.
- Resolves conflicts to the benefit all the parties.
- Celebrates team accomplishments.
- Fosters interpersonal relationships for diversity of thought.
- Encourages community involvement.
- Manages by walking around, asking, "How can I serve you?"
- Maintains an open-door policy.
- Conducts performance reviews as self-evaluations.

- Allows employees to make decisions that affect their work.

"We should not let our fears hold us back from pursuing our hope."
—John F. Kennedy

Interpersonal Skills in a Fear-Free Workplace

How do employees use their interpersonal skills in a workplace without fear? Remember that how we use our skills comes from our learned behavior, and that our behavior is shaped by our personality. We are on "automatic pilot" most of the time, and it takes awareness and an acknowledgement of how we are currently behaving in order to change our behavior. It might be helpful to ask yourself the following questions about your workplace:

- How do employees communicate with one another?
- How are decisions made?
- How is conflict resolved?

- How are employees inspired?
- How do employees embrace change?
- How do employees participate on teams?

How Does the Use of Interpersonal Skills Impact an Organization's Performance?

Managers in a fear-free environment use their interpersonal skills differently than they would in a culture of fear. They communicate the vision of the organization openly to the employees, resolve conflicts and solve problems for the benefit of all employees, foster consensus thinking, and engage everyone to participate in the change process. These managers inspire teams to go beyond just getting the job done by making an emotional appeal and connecting with the members on a higher level. They have a high level of emotional intelligence and exhibit compassion and empathy for everyone. These managers are authentic and genuine, and they use power and influence to provide resources and forge relationships. Remember Maslow's Hierarchy of Needs? These managers want all their employees to be at the highest level possible.

> *"There is no place for fear in the workplace.*
> *It destroys trust and inhibits organizational*
> *change in good and difficult times."*
> —Jack Lowe (former CEO of TD Industries)

Change begins when employees consciously commit to building a high trust, high-performance workplace, focusing on each other's strengths rather than on weaknesses. To build a high trust, high-performance workplace, organizations must provide support for employees at all levels to learn to use their interpersonal skills constructively. The ultimate goal is to identify and embrace the behaviors at every level that promote trust and manage and reduce fear. "Trust is a function of two things: character and competence. Character includes integrity, your motives with people. Competence includes your capabilities, your skills, your results, your track record. And both are vital." (Covey, 2006)

Now that you've had a chance to review two different workplaces (one with fear and one without fear) and the characteristics of managers in those workplaces, how would you characterize your workplace?

_____

_____

_____

Personal Reflection

What events occur in your workplace that create trust or fear in the employees? What have you personally experienced?

_____

_____

_____

_____

Which employees in your workplace stimulate fear or build trust in others?

_____

_____

_____

_____

_____

_____

What do these employees say or do? What will you do differently at work to build trust?

_____

_____

_____

_____

_____

_____

Summary of Chapter 1

This chapter compared workplaces and mangers that promote a fear-free culture with those that foster a fear-based culture, giving examples of how managers might use their interpersonal skills in these two environments. It also provided descriptions and examples of fear-based behaviors and those that build trust in the workplace. The chapter provides many insights into the characteristics of these managers and a forum to openly and honestly discuss fear with colleagues and employees. From your own experience, no doubt you can think of many more characteristics of both types of workplaces and managers. This chapter creates an awarenss of fear in the workplace and its impact on organizational effectiveness.

Your Reflections About Chapter 1

_____

_____

_____

_____

_____

_____

_____

_____

_____

_____

_____

_____

_____

_____

Chapter 2

Symptoms of Fear

~~~

The most destructive factor in the human mind is fear.

—Gladys Moore

Fear can affect the decisions and choices we make, both personally and professionally. This chapter describes the symptoms and patterns of behaviors that occur when fear is in control of the mind. The best way to explain this is by comparing the mind to the functions of a computer.

How the Mind Works

The metaphor of a computer demonstrates how the mind functions. The computer has a processor and hard drive. When programmed correctly, a computer is easy to use and allows you to input and retrieve information, providing you follow the correct operating procedure. If you don't follow the correct procedure, you may get an error message that says, "You have performed an illegal operation; please exit the program" (Figure 6). In some cases, the computer may become contaminated with a virus and stop working.

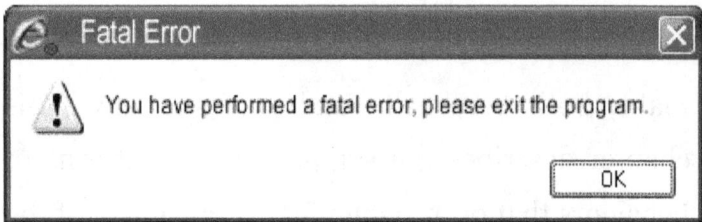

Figure 6 –Fatal Error (Computer)

The mind functions in a manner similar to a computer. The processor (the conscious or "power" part of the mind) receives information and records it on your "hard drive" (the memory or subconscious part of the mind). When you respond to something you see, hear, feel, or need, the power or conscious part retrieves the information from your subconscious or memory. That is the normal function of the mind. However, when fear is introduced, it can act like a virus that controls the power part, distorting the operating system. Your personal error message is, "You have lost your peace of mind" (Figure 7). Fear is the virus in the mind, and the information you receive when it is running is all fear-based.

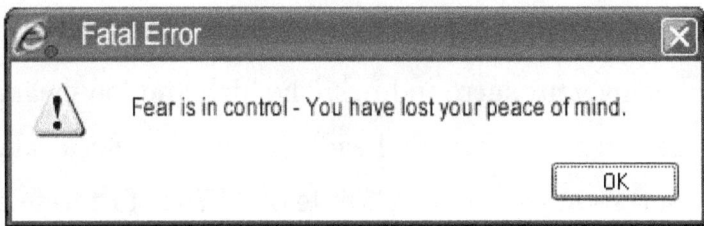

```
┌─────────────────────────────────────────────────────┐
│ 🅮  Fatal Error                                    ☒ │
├─────────────────────────────────────────────────────┤
│  ⚠   Fear is in control - You have lost your peace of mind. │
│                                                       │
│                               ┌──────────────┐        │
│                               │      OK       │        │
│                               └──────────────┘        │
└─────────────────────────────────────────────────────┘
```

Figure 7 –Fatal Error (Mind)

The Fog of Fear

To better understand this idea, picture in your mind a beautiful day. The sun is warm and the air is humid. As evening falls and the sun sets, the temperature starts to drop, making for a magnificent drive to your final destination. As you continue on your journey, you notice it gets a bit harder to see—visibility is reduced to a few hundred feet as fog descends on the two-lane road you have traveled many times before. You proceed, expecting the fog to clear in the next mile or two, as it has in the past. As you continue driving, you find it difficult to recognize signs, lane markers, oncoming traffic, exits, and the lights from the surrounding communities. You slow down because you are having difficulty seeing your surroundings. The high and low-beam settings on the car's headlights don't help at all, and soon you are in a "white out." You start to feel anxious—concerned for your safety and the safety of others. You have lost all sense of where you are. As you continue to creep along, you realize the conditions are not going to improve. A gradual condition has slowly progressed to create a frightening experience. You feel paralyzed and are not sure what to do. You stop the car and wait.

Psychological fear—the feeling of being rejected or inadequate—can create the same conditions as the fog. You may feel paralyzed and become immobile, responding negatively to situations and becoming defensive, withdrawn, or vindictive. The feeling of fear can creep up on you just as the fog did, without much warning. If you continue to ignore the signs, you can become consumed with fear, and all your responses and actions are based upon dealing with the fear. You end up just as you did in the fog—not knowing which way to turn.

Where Does Fear Come From? What Stimulates Fear in Our Lives?

Fear can be stimulated in our relationships with others when we are judged harshly, criticized unjustly, or challenged unfairly, leading us to feel *rejected or inadequate*. It can be stimulated by seeing or experiencing something or someone: a tragic event, an abusive manager, the loss of a promotion, or even being asked to speak in front of a group.

When we feel rejected or inadequate—and if we allow the psychological fear of rejection or inadequacy to control our responses negatively—the power or conscious part of the mind (the processor) will retrieve from our memory or subconscious (hard drive) only the information on how to respond with fear. It can happen in an instant, and usually is triggered by something we see, feel, hear, or need. It is a very powerful yet simple concept.

Fear responses may include:

- Physical reactions such as clenching your jaw, feeling knots in your stomach, or experiencing a rapid heart rate.
- Becoming irrational in your thinking and unclear in your judgment.
- Experiencing a state of confusion as you attempt to cope with the feeling.

- Becoming defensive, perhaps verbally attacking the person that stimulated your feeling of rejection or inadequacy.

"With irrational fear of rejection and inadequacy, we psych ourselves out." (Roselle, 2006) Do you recall the vignettes in Chapter 1? Go back and review them, noticing if the participants responded negatively in the situations where they felt rejected or inadequate. Review the descriptions of workplaces and managers that stimulate fear. Recognize that when we respond negatively in such situations, we are responding with fear.

"We need to change the way we use our mind
so it works better."
—Gladys Moore

Examples of Fear Situations

Following are accounts of fear situations I have been personally aware of, which demonstrate how fear controls the mind and reveal typical responses that occur when we feel rejected or inadequate. Such responses usually are based on something we **see, hear, feel, or need**.

See: I witnessed a senior executive verbally attack and abuse a co-worker of mine for a mistake made in a report. The executive threw the report across the room and threatened my co-worker with the loss of a promotion if such a mistake ever happened again. The meeting ended abruptly, with the senior executive leaving the office.

Astounded at what I had witnessed, I felt inadequate in this situation because I was unable to console my colleague. I became frustrated and angry to the point that I didn't respond to customer phone calls for over a week. I vowed never to take a risk or make a mistake, saying to myself, "I will do everything by the book and nothing more." Was this the correct way for me to respond in that situation? In retrospect, I think not. When the fear of being inadequate controls our responses, we can become emotional and irrational in our thinking.

Hear: For over 11 years, I had reported directly to the president of the company I worked for. We worked well together, but as the company grew from 20 to 60 employees, a vice president was hired to manage the team, and I was to report to him. I had heard he was a very difficult person to work for and demonstrated controlling behavior. In his new role, he chose the projects I would work on, often leaving me out of critical meetings with the president. I felt *rejected and inadequate* and started questioning what I had done to deserve this type of treatment. Rather than confronting him directly, I began to doubt myself and worry that I might not be doing a good job. My self-esteem was starting to diminish, even though I had been very successful in the past.

Can you sense the fear creeping into my mind? With fear controlling the power part (processor), what kind of information was I likely to receive from my memory (hard drive)? In my mind, I started defending my feelings that I should determine the projects I would work on and be included in all meetings that involved my work. It only seemed fair, as I had been with the company longer than the vice president had. This type of thinking went on for several weeks and was affecting my performance. Finally, I decided to have a conversation with the vice president to address how I felt. He acknowledged my feelings and said he would be more thoughtful in the future.

Feel: Several years ago, I thought I deserved a promotion because I met all the requirements for a new position in my workplace, yet I was passed over because my manager did not want to lose me to another department. I was angry and didn't speak to the manager for days. I felt inadequate and rejected, and it showed in my performance. Because I was unable to do anything about the situation, I felt helpless and alone. I began questioning whether I wanted to work for the company any longer and distanced myself from co-workers and customers. Finally, I left the company.

Need: The corporate office of a company I was working for announced there would be a 20% reduction in the workforce. I had recently married, just purchased a home, and was paying off several loans. Clearly, I needed my job. I thought, "How am I going to survive with all the bills? How will I buy groceries and pay the utilities?" The concern was greater because my wife and I didn't have savings. Since I had recently been hired, I felt victimized and angry, and also felt inadequate for not having money saved for a time like this. Stressed to the point that I could hardly eat, I started asking myself, "Should I look for a new job now, or wait?" My mind was completely controlled by fear. Even if I had received information about what to do, I would have negated it. My thoughts, feelings, and emotions were focused so intensely on fears about the future that I did not have clarity about what actions I should take. My fear caused me to assume the worst-case scenario.

These are the types of experiences we can encounter at any time. What is important is how we respond not only these situations, but to many other challenges we may face. Responding negatively indicates that we are responding with fear.

What challenging experiences can you recall? How might you respond differently from the way you did?

_____

_____

_____

_____

Your mind functions similarly to a computer. In Figure 8, the circles represent the conscious and subconscious aspects of the mind. The conscious portion is the "power" part of the mind (your processor). It receives information from what you see, hear, feel, and need as you experience each day. This information is recorded on your "hard drive" (memory or subconscious), which acts as a storage unit for all your experiences. It records everything without distinguishing between "good or bad" (valid or invalid) information. When you respond to something you see, hear, feel, or need, the power (conscious) part retrieves the information from your subconscious (memory). This is the normal, natural function of the mind and how it works, and is quite straightforward. If, for example, I ask you how much is one plus one, your immediate response is "two." You responded to something you heard through the conscious mind and immediately retrieved the answer from the subconscious. It happened in an instant, didn't it? That shows how powerfully and quickly the mind functions.

Figure 8 shows how the mind functions without fear, in its normal and natural state. It is the way the mind should function in every situation we are faced with, either personally or professionally.

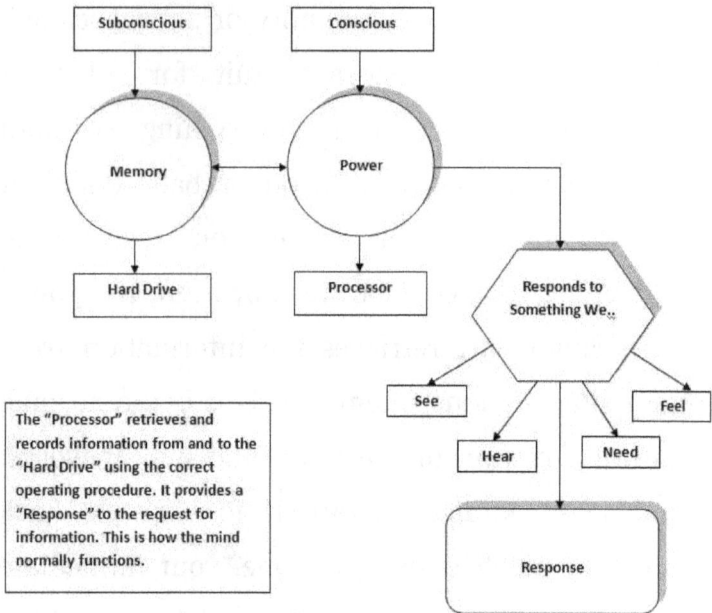

Subconscious

Conscious

Memory

Power

Hard Drive

Processor

Responds to Something We...

See

Feel

Hear

Need

The "Processor" retrieves and records information from and to the "Hard Drive" using the correct operating procedure. It provides a "Response" to the request for information. This is how the mind normally functions.

Response

Figure 8 – The Mind As a Computer

If, however, you respond to information or a situation in the workplace when the psychological fear of feeling rejected or inadequate is controlling the conscious or power part of the mind—and if you respond negatively to such things as change, public speaking, uncertainty, a layoff, a new manager, and so forth—then-fear is distorting the operating system. In such situations, your personal error message is, "You have lost your peace of mind." Fear becomes the virus in the mind, and the information you receive is all fear-based. When the power part of your mind is controlled by fear, it can retrieve only fear-based information from your memory—it's that simple. The following workplace scenario illustrates this concept.

Mark (who had demonstrated great skills and knowledge in his job) worked hard for a promotion his manager assured him he would receive, but later was told that the promotion was given to a colleague. Mark can respond to this news in several ways. One choice would be to accept the decision, consider other options, and continue to stay focused in his role even though he is disappointed. Another alternative is to respond negatively to the decision—feeling rejected and inadequate due to the fear of failure or loss, and becoming angry and vindictive toward his manager, colleagues, and customers.

In the second scenario, fear controls his responses—Mark withdraws his energy and vows never to work that hard again. In this case, what is the impact on his future performance? Is there trust left in the relationship with his manager? How is Mark likely to use his interpersonal skills in the future? Think about various other scenarios that exist in today's workplace. What is the impact of a culture of fear on an organization?

In everyday living, when we respond to what we see, hear, feel, and need without fear controlling the mind, our response is normal and we move on to the next situation. However, when we respond to someone or something we encounter with feelings of rejection or inadequacy, becoming angry or hateful, it is apparent that we are responding with fear. Using fear as a coping mechanism may lead to behaviors such as withdrawing, becoming defensive, criticizing, controlling, being vindictive, and becoming closed minded.

Figure 9 illustrates what happens when fear controls the mind.

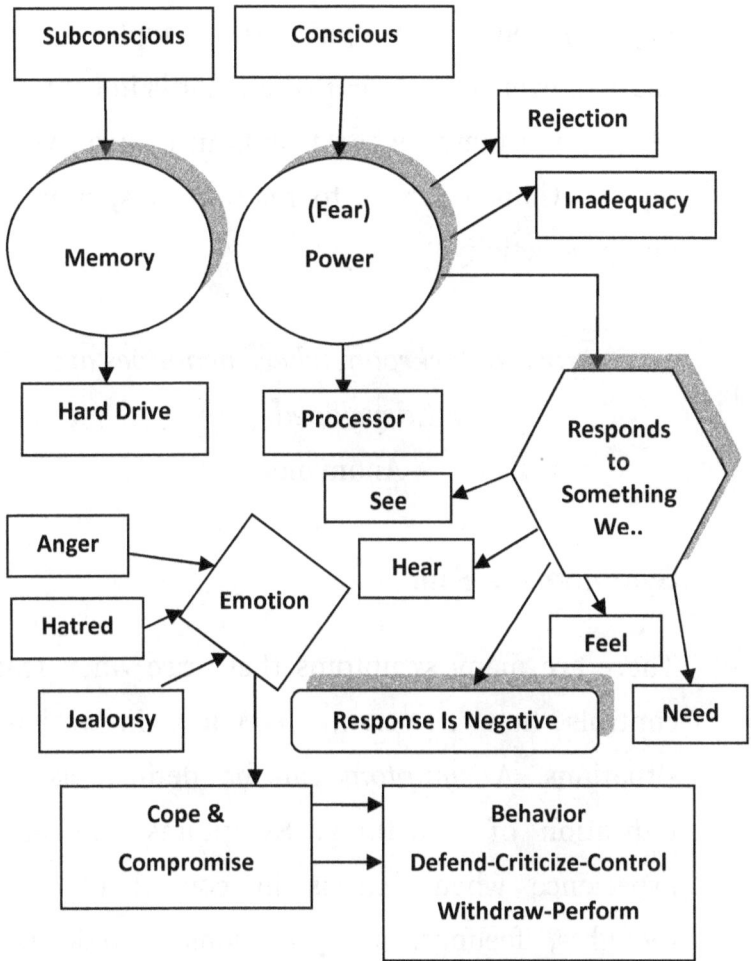

Figure 9 – The Mind When Fear Is in Control

Notice the differences between Figure 8 and Figure 9. Do you recognize the symptoms and chain of events that occur when fear is in control? More importantly, when fear is in control, what do you think happens to relationships, morale, and productivity?

> *"Fear is a darkroom where negatives are developed."*
>
> —Anonymous

Symptoms of Fear

There are many symptoms that arise when fear controls how a person responds in various situations. A *symptom* can be defined as an indication of something. Symptoms you may experience when fear is in control of your thoughts, feelings, and emotions include the following:

Agitated	Jealous	Nervous
Anxious	Worried	Annoyed
Irritated	Apprehensive	Vengeful
Angry	Hateful	Doubtful

Let's use the feeling of *doubt* to make a point. How often have you heard someone say, "I can't come up with the right answer to the problem," or, "I doubt my voice will be heard at the next staff meeting"? Such statements are symptoms that fear may be in control of the power part of the mind. If these symptoms continue unchecked and the fear of feeling rejected or inadequate remains, the person may develop a behavior to cope with their fear. These behaviors are very destructive and can destroy relationships, both personal and professional.

Look at the following list of fear-based behaviors. Behaviors when fear is in control include being:

Defensive	Withdrawn	A Know-It-All
A Victim	A Performer	A Habitual Liar
A Controller	Critical	Vindictive
A Blamer	Argumentative	An Avoider
Closed-Minded	Compulsive	Aggressive
A Perfectionist	A Procrastinator	Guilty

You may have personally experienced some of these behaviors or recognized them in others. Have you noticed any of these symptoms and behaviors in your workplace? When employees act this way, it makes it very difficult for them to be productive and engaged in their work.

It isn't always possible to eliminate the feeling of being rejected or inadequate, but you can change how you respond to that feeling. When fear-based behaviors arise in the workplace, they often distract employees and managers from making crucial decisions. After experiencing angry behavior from a co-worker or manager, employees tend to choose the most expeditious route to work around that person. They may comply with their demands, but often it is only lip service. "The most effective day-to-day responses you make are informed by the heart and your cortex working in concert with each other. This cannot happen when you are beset by fears and faulty beliefs that undermine your confidence and block your ability to think clearly." (Roselle, 2006)

> *"No passion so effectively robs the mind of all of its powers of acting and reasoning as fear."*
> —Edmund Burke (18th-century philosopher)

People, events, and situations may lead you to feel rejected or inadequate. Which of the following circumstances can you relate to? Remember that the important thing is how you respond to them. If you respond negatively (with anger, hatred, or jealousy), you are responding with fear.

Professional Life

	Rejected	Inadequate
A manager or supervisor	_____	_____
A co-worker	_____	_____
A difficult task	_____	_____
A new policy	_____	_____
A performance review	_____	_____
A new position	_____	_____
Being left out of a meeting	_____	_____
Office politics	_____	_____
Lack of recognition	_____	_____
Being micromanaged	_____	_____
Derogatory remarks	_____	_____
Unrealistic deadlines	_____	_____
Too many projects	_____	_____

Personal Life

	Rejected	Inadequate
Change	_____	_____
Growing old	_____	_____
Public speaking	_____	_____
Making a mistake	_____	_____
Divorce	_____	_____
Losing a loved one	_____	_____
Appearance	_____	_____
Family member	_____	_____
Friend	_____	_____
Loss of a job	_____	_____
Lack of money	_____	_____
Not feeling loved	_____	_____
Not meeting expectations	_____	_____

There are many things you see, hear, feel, and need that can lead you to feel rejected or inadequate. However, it is how you respond to them—either with or without fear—that determines how well your mind works.

What Can I Do About This? How Can I Change?

There is a solution to managing and reducing fear in your life and in the workplace. When you experience such symptoms and feel rejected or inadequate, you can simply say or think, "Release my fear" and ask for "peace of mind." Change your thoughts to positive affirmations. Your mind will follow and give you the guidance on how to respond in difficult situations. I know it sounds too simple; however, it does work! The key is in changing your thoughts. Feeling rejected or inadequate is a normal feeling, but you can change how you respond to that feeling.

Following is a six-step ACTION process (the acronym comes from the first letter of the first word of each step) that provides a way to address feeling rejected or inadequate and to release your fear. The mind functions in a simple way. By following this process, you can change the way you respond to difficult situations.

ACTION Process

Step 1	**A**cknowledge your thoughts, feelings, emotions, and the information you experience daily. They are real.
Step 2	**C**oncede that when you respond negatively to someone or something (with anger, hatred or jealousy), you are responding with fear. Fear is in control of your mind.
Step 3	**T**ell your mind to *"release the fear"* to receive the appropriate guidance. You may have to do it several times.
Step 4	**I**nvite the guidance the mind gives you. If you don't know what to do—or when or how to do it—that is your guidance. Use the guidance and depend upon it. No action is called for at this time.
Step 5	**O**bserve and be aware that you are coping and compromising with fear when you start negating the guidance with thoughts that include words like *maybe, could have, should have, or can't*. These are indicators that you are not using your mind correctly. Release your fear again if you find you are still using these indicators.
Step 6	**N**ote that the experience will be stored in your memory without fear. The next time the mind accesses this experience from your memory, you will not have to deal with the fear.

Releasing fear is a powerful and transformational skill that must be practiced to become a natural part of your thought process. Be aware that when you respond to someone or something negatively (with anger, hatred, or jealousy), it is an indication that you are responding with fear. Make a simple adjustment and ask the mind to *"release your fear."* The process is that simple and effective. Your mind without fear will provide guidance regarding the appropriate steps to take, which likely will involve things for you to do or say. Rely on this guidance; it will keep you safe. This powerful discipline will allow you to trust yourself and build trusting relationships with others.

When you are free of fear, a whole new world opens up. You no longer will be afraid of making a mistake, encountering closed-door meetings, taking a risk, experiencing change, facing the unknown, meeting expectations, growing old, losing a job, speaking up at a meeting, or even having a conversation with an abusive employee. The discipline of releasing fear will enable you to respond to the challenges (both personal and professional) you encounter each day.

Thought Changers

Once you have followed the six-step ACTION process, you also can redirect your thoughts. Following is a list of "thought changers" that are useful for experiencing inner peace in the workplace. You may not succeed with the first attempt, but if you continue saying these affirmations earnestly, you will gradually begin to experience peace of mind.

- I have handled difficult situations in the past with great results.
- I expect to have peace of mind, and for a solution to be there when I need it.
- It's not me they are upset with; it's the issue.
- I expect to have clarity in making decisions.
- It's okay to make a mistake; I will learn from it.

- I will focus on the successes, not the failures.
- I look for the good in everyone and respect each individual as a person.
- I choose joy and peace versus anger and hatred.
- I am grateful for the caring relationships I have, and will focus on these when confronted with abusiveness.
- This thought I am having is of no value, so I will let it go.
- This conversation is going nowhere, so I choose not to continue to engage in it.
- I don't need to solve this problem right now; I will come back to it.
- I deserve respect and consideration, and I accept it right now.
- I focus on my positive qualities, traits, and strengths.
- I trust my intuition to make the right choice.

- I don't need to control everything and always be right; I let go of ego.

Practice the six-step ACTION process to release fear and maintain your peace of mind. Identify the "thought changers" that work for you. Remember to practice this skill repeatedly until it becomes a normal and natural habit.

Personal Reflection

What are your symptoms and behaviors when you are allowing fear to control how you respond?

_____

_____

_____

_____

_____

_____

How do your fear-based symptoms and behaviors affect your co-workers?

_____

_____

_____

_____

_____

_____

What is the impact of your fear-based behaviors and responses on your department and the organization?

_____

_____

_____

_____

_____

_____

Thomas J. Yagos

The Far-Reaching Effects of Workplace Fear

Fear-based behaviors often are the tip of the iceberg in an organization (Figure 10). It's very difficult to see what goes on below the surface because the reasons for the results are hidden from view. If an organization has a fear-based culture, the work environment becomes very difficult to function in, leading to a decline in organizational performance. Over time, fear erodes the relationships, and the visible portion of the iceberg continues to grow.

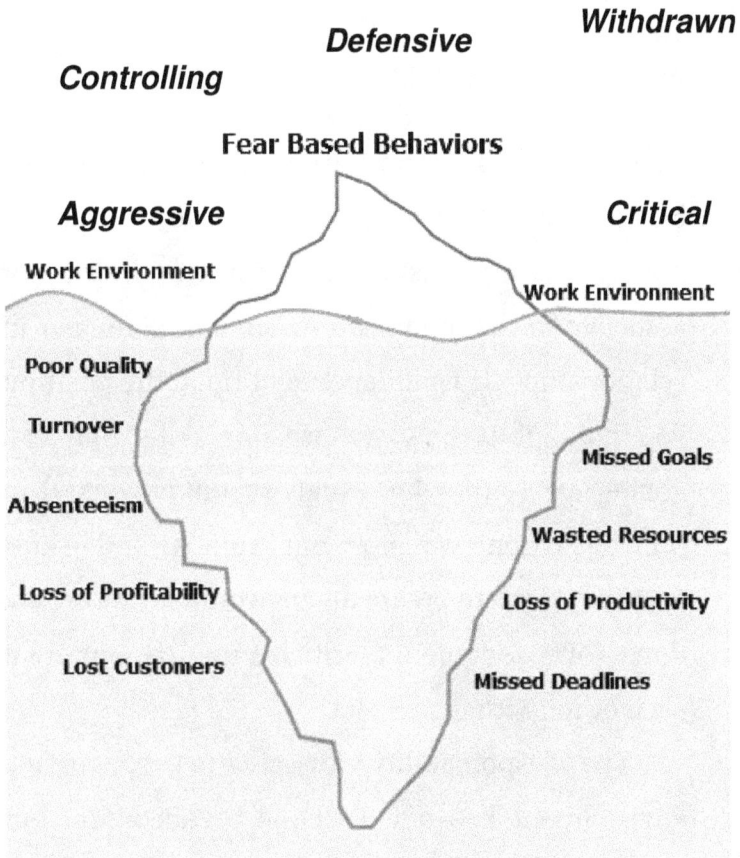

Withdrawn

Defensive

Controlling

Fear Based Behaviors

Aggressive   *Critical*

Work Environment

Work Environment

Poor Quality

Turnover

Missed Goals

Absenteeism

Wasted Resources

Loss of Profitability

Loss of Productivity

Lost Customers

Missed Deadlines

Figure 10 – Far-Reaching Effects of
Workplace Fear

Thomas J. Yagos

The New Discipline to Eliminate Fear

How Do I Change?

Remember that organizations don't create fear-based workplaces; employees do. A CEO, manager, supervisor, department head, or associate in the organization can stimulate fear in relationships. It isn't dependent upon the position you hold; it is how we use our skills that can create fear (either knowingly or unknowingly) in others. When we use our minds and skills correctly, we can create an environment where we don't form judgments, criticize unjustly, or treat each other with disrespect.

The responsibility for creating a trusting environment lies not with the organization, but with each of its members. "When leaders create trusting working environments, people are safe to challenge the system and perform beyond expectations. Employees feel more freedom to express their creative ideas. They are more willing to take risks, admit mistakes, and learn from the mistakes." (Renia & Renia, 1999)

The Tool for Breaking the Cycle of Fear in the Workplace

Remember that when you respond to someone or something negatively, you are responding with fear. Anger, hatred, jealousy, and blaming are indicators that you are responding negatively. Make a simple adjustment and ask the mind to *"release your fear."* Without fear, your mind will receive information about the appropriate steps to take.

Use the ACTION process and thought-changers to maintain your peace of mind. The legacy of fear will be broken when organizations acknowledge the existence of fear and talk about it. To do this successfully, we must first understand that fear exists within ourselves. As we increase our awareness of fear and its impact on relationships, it enables us to become a role model in the organization and help others build self-awareness. We can identify what creates fear and what builds trust, enlisting support from others to do the same.

What Will You Do Differently Each Day?

In many organizations, a fundamental shift must take place to create a culture that supports inspired and engaged employees. When an organization takes steps to eliminate fear and build trust, the level of employee engagement increases. Trust bonds personal relationships; fear destroys them.

High-performing organizations understand that reducing and managing fear is necessary to create an environment of high trust and performance, the ingredients for sustaining the organization. "Fearless leadership is not the absence of fear. It's the courage to confront fear and solve the problems from a radically new direction." (Malandro, 2009)

What is the legacy you would like to leave personally and professionally in the workplace? The intent to live your life without fear opens up endless opportunities. Following are examples of the benefits:

- Developing a trusting relationship with yourself.

- Being respectful, honest, and considerate of others.

- Inspiring others by serving as an example for building trusting relationships.

- Using your interpersonal skills in a caring manner, without judgment or criticism.

How Will These Changes Impact the Organization?

The benefits of an organization without fear can be described "as inspired individuals developing inspired teams, leading to an inspired community."

What would a 5% increase in productivity mean to you, your team, and the organization? If you believe that a culture of trust will improve productivity, profitability, quality, customer service, performance, and engagement, then you must manage and eliminate fear in the workplace. This is how high-performing organizations are transforming the workplace with a new vision: a workplace free of fear where relationships are built on a foundation of trust. Change your mind, and you can change your life.

Knowledge of this concept without application wastes the potential of a great mind. "Building trust requires attention to every aspect of the firm's design—its structure, management policies and practices, technological systems, informal culture, the values and expectations of its members, and the behavior of those in leadership positions." (Shaw, 1997)

Summary of Chapter 2

This chapter used the metaphor of comparing the functions of the mind to the functions of a computer. The diagrams illustrated the process of how the mind operates when it is not controlled by fear and when it is controlled by fear. Lists of symptoms and behaviors that typically occur when fear controls the mind were presented. Methods for shifting from fear states were provided, including a six-step ACTION process to release fear and a list of "thought-changers" to help sustain the change. Chapter 2 demonstrated that releasing fear is a powerful skill for building both personal and professional relationships.

Your Reflections About Chapter 2

_____

_____

_____

_____

_____

_____

_____

_____

_____

_____

_____

Thomas J. Yagos

Chapter 3

Creating a Fear-Free Culture

~~~

*The experience of overcoming fear is
extraordinarily delightful.*

—Bertrand Russell

Let's examine several workplace scenarios to
determine if fear exists by looking at the
behaviors of the individuals and the outcomes for
the organization. Reflect on some of the concepts
you have learned in this book. As you review the
scenarios, think about the symptoms and
behaviors of the participants. How does fear
manifest itself in their behaviors?

Communication

Communication, a core skill, allows people to
share and exchange information, influences

attitudes and behaviors, and even shapes personalities. What we say to someone and how we say it can make a deep and lasting impression. What impression do you want to make with your communication skills?

Using your mind correctly in the communication process is crucial to building relationships based on trust. Good communication entails presenting information, ideas, and feelings in a nonthreatening way, without being judgmental or attacking another person. If we use our minds correctly, we can communicate without rejecting the other person or making them feel inadequate. We are capable of doing that when fear doesn't control our mind. How we communicate with others does influence behavior, as you will observe in the following scenario.

Scenario — Speaking Up at Staff Meetings

Think about the employee or manager that dominates a meeting with little respect for someone else's ideas. They often dismiss others without consideration or interest in their contributions. If employees speak up, this type of person chastises or ridicules them in front of the group. When this happens, employees are no longer responsive and feel uncomfortable expressing ideas and their true feelings about a subject.

Alex was an aggressive general manager of a printing company, who conducted staff meetings that focused on getting right to the point. He asked for ideas from his staff about operational issues; however, when they attempted to respond to his questions, they were told their ideas were ridiculous and not related to the topic. Following is an example of an interaction between Alex and Louis, the operations manager, that in occurred in a meeting.

Alex (General Manager): We are experiencing significant cost overruns on current customer orders. What are you going to do about it?

Louis (Operations Manager): The cost of paper has increased by five percent in the last six months. Has the price increase been accounted for in customer proposals?

Alex: Don't you think I am smart enough to include that in the proposals, Louis?

Louis: I was asking the question to determine what steps we can take to reduce operating costs. Looking at the cost of material is the first place to start. As the general manager, you should know that. Are you sure your sales team is pricing the products correctly?

Alex: There are surely more thoughtful questions than that! What about the labor costs on the jobs? Are you sure you didn't make a mistake on your original quotes to me?

Louis: I think we should brainstorm for ideas on how to get the costs in line with the proposals. We have some very experienced plant managers in this meeting who have some ideas about reducing costs.

John (Plant Supervisor): I have done some research on another paper supplier and found that we can reduce our costs.

Alex: I don't think brainstorming will help at this point. I knew I should have taken matters into my own hands! Here is what I think you need to do to fix the problem. [He hands Louis a piece of paper.] I expect to see better results in the next week, or heads will roll. Is there anything else that needs to be discussed before you get back to work?

Louis: Let's take at least another 15 minutes to hear other ideas these managers have.

Alex: I have another meeting to attend.

Alex left, and Louis overheard the managers making comments as they exited the meeting.

Their overall reaction was, "Why should we bother? Alex doesn't respect us or our ideas. He does everything his way. What's the use? We did all that work for nothing."

Take a few moments to answer the following questions:

What type of behavior was exhibited by Alex and Louis?

_____

_____

_____

What are the reasons for these types of behaviors?

_____

_____

_____

What was the outcome of the meeting for the two participants in the conversation?

_____

_____

How did the other participants in the meeting react to the conversation?

_____

_____

What do you think the result of the meeting was for the company and its customers?

_____

_____

What tool do we have to eliminate fear and maintain our peace of mind?

_____

_____

Without fear in control, what might Alex or Louis have said differently?

_____

_____

_____

What is the effect of criticizing, judging, and challenging employees in meetings?

_____

_____

_____

What is the underlying factor that controls these types of behaviors?

_____

_____

_____

The Underlying Factor

If you identified the underlying factor as "the fear of feeling rejected or inadequate," you were correct.

If you were either participant in this scenario (Alex or Louis), what steps would you take to maintain your peace of mind?

_____

_____

_____

_____

_____

_____

_____

Conflict Resolution

Conflicts that occur in our personal and professional lives can range from where to have dinner, to how to teach our children, to what to wear to work, to how to discipline an employee.

4332

The list can go on forever! Conflict is a part of human nature, and most of us have difficulty dealing with conflicts for a variety of personal reasons. Yet, resolving conflicts in the workplace is a critical interpersonal skill. Employees know that handling conflict well with a boss, fellow employee, or client can improve relationships and enhance the organization's image.

Conflicts may arise due to differences in opinions, experiences, or ideas. How we respond to conflicts is critical to maintaining the integrity of the relationships involved. The following scenario between Tom and Bill illustrates this point.

Scenario — Values

Bill, a sales associate of a technology company, knew his sales had been flat for the past two months and that there was constant pressure from investors about performance. To meet the sales targets for the business, Gerry, his sales manager, was pressuring Bill to ship equipment to a client even though the client couldn't use it. The client agreed to hold the merchandise in their warehouse for 30 days, which would help boost Bill's month-end sales revenue. After the month was closed, Gerry would ask the customer to return the merchandise. Bill knew what Gerry was doing and struggled with the idea of reporting the numbers to his manager. After Gerry had threatened Bill on several occasions that he could lose his job, Bill decided to confront him. Following is an account of their conversation.

Bill: I know I'm behind in sales for this month. I hope next month will generate additional business to give comfort to the investors. In the meantime, I have a problem with reporting sales numbers that are not accurate. I'm not going to be dishonest. Just tell the investors the truth!

Gerry: We can't wait for next month, Bill. We need to report our projected figures, or the investors will reduce the financing for the company. I need you to ship the merchandise immediately to the client. I know you have a family and rely on the income from this job. If you want your job, you had better ship the merchandise! I also think you should be working longer hours to improve sales results.

Bill: The territory you gave me will not support the sales targets for the merchandise! Also, I didn't receive the proper training for this job, and our prices are much higher than our competitors' prices. I just don't feel good about shipping the merchandise, and I resent your comment about working longer hours! I am already working 50 to 60 hours a week. I don't think you were totally truthful with me about this position when you hired me a year ago. Telling the truth seems to be a problem for you. Why don't *you* ship the merchandise? What are you concerned about? You have the authorization to do it.

Gerry: You ship the merchandise this time, and I will see about getting you a bigger territory and more training.

Bill: Thank you, but it doesn't feel right, and it's dishonest to misinform the investors about our sales revenue. What will happen if they find out?

Gerry: Do you want work here?

Bill: But—

Gerry: Just do it!

Bill went back to his office, made arrangements to ship the merchandise, and resented his decision. Extremely upset, he was unable to concentrate on anything else for the rest of the day.

Take a few moments to answer the following questions.

What type of behavior was exhibited by Gerry and Bill?

_____

_____

_____

What are the reasons for these types of behaviors?

_____

_____

_____

What was the outcome of the meeting for the two participants in the conversation?

_____

_____

_____

What do you think the result of the meeting was for the company and its clients?

_____

_____

_____

What tools do we have to eliminate fear and maintain our peace of mind?

_____

_____

_____

Without fear in control, what could Gerry or Bill have said differently?

_____

_____

_____

How would you describe the values in this organization?

_____

_____

What is the underlying factor that controls these types of behaviors?

_____

_____

The Underlying Factor

If you identified the underlying factor as "the fear of feeling rejected or inadequate," you were correct.

If you were either participant in this scenario, what steps would you take to maintain your peace of mind?

As you can understand from reading the two scenarios, these types of behaviors exist in organizations. Such fear-based behaviors must be called to people's attention, managed, reduced, and eliminated in order to improve relationships—and more importantly, to improve productivity and reduce the costs I previously identified.

Action Plan

The final part of this book leads you through the development of a personal action plan. When you want to achieve something significant and sustain the learning, the best approach is to develop a personal action plan and teach others what you have learned.

The retention rate shown in Figure 11 for new information after 48 hours is based on the adult learning model. To use the ACTION process to make changes in your life, practice it daily with your family, friends, and colleagues, and teach them the skill of releasing fear. Over time this skill will become second-nature to how you behave, both personally and professionally.

	Average Retention Rates
A Lecture	5%
Reading	10%
An Audio-Visual Presentation	20%
A Demonstration	30%
A Discussion Group	50%
Practice by Doing	75%
Teaching Others to Use	80%

Institute of Applied Behavioral Sciences

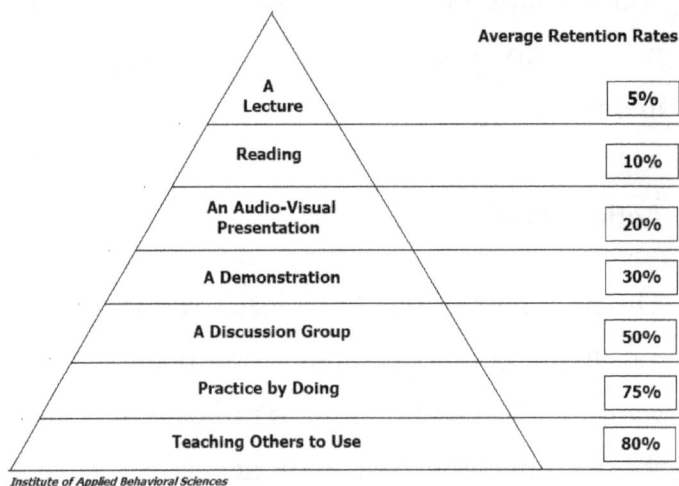

Figure 11 —-Retention Rates
(Institute of Applied Behavioral Sciences)

Build the plan not only to inspire yourself, but to inspire others. Identify just three initiatives or changes you would like to accomplish. Based on your understanding of how fear can impact you personally and professionally, determine how you will use your skills in each area to eliminate fear and build trust. Make the plan realistic, and hold yourself accountable for implementing the changes.

Engage others in your action plan. Express your interest in hearing how you are doing in workplace situations. Be honest! Ask thoughtful questions, and let others know you want to change your behavior and need their support. Be open-minded to the feedback you receive. Look at things from two perspectives: one based on fear and one based on trust.

Before you develop your personal action plan, review the characteristics of workplaces and managers that focus on building trust and eliminating fear in the workplace. Where do you fall on the continuum between fear and trust?

Creating Your Plan: Moving From a Place of Fear to Trust

Change starts with you! Develop changes in your behavior that will build trust. Create your plan using the following five steps.

Step 1 – Identify Changes

Choose changes that are important to you and your colleagues.

Focus on no more than three changes you are personally committed to.

Describe what you will do from a positive point of view.

Think in terms of your behavior rather than business results.

Make the changes clear enough so that others can tell if they are achieved.

Example: I will conduct staff meetings so that everyone is allowed to share their ideas and be heard. I will thank the participants.

Use the following guidelines so you will you know when you have made the changes:

Clearly describe the new behaviors or skills you wish to develop.

Define success in making the changes with criteria that are specific, measurable or observable, realistic, and with a timeline.

Once you have developed a statement of success criteria, ask for feedback from others about the statement.

Step 2 – Identify Action Steps
(Implement something every day)

Select action steps that will help you be successful.

Choose either personal or professional activities.

Tailor your action steps to your learning style.

Integrate action steps into processes, events, and tasks you are already doing.

Include action steps to practice behaviors with specific groups or in particular situations.

Look for activities for which you are directly responsible for the outcome.

Specify steps you will take to hold yourself accountable and encourage others to hold you accountable for your changes.

Step 3 – Plan Time for Reflection
(Reflect on what happens)

Build time into your routine to reflect on what you are learning and ask yourself questions such as: What's working? What's not working? How will I do things differently the next time?

Determine how you will remind yourself to take a few minutes to reflect.

Establish how you will track what you are learning. You may want to keep notes in a journal or track your progress in an electronic document.

Example: Take a few minutes after work each day to think about what you tried, what went well, what didn't go well, and what you will do differently next time. Think about the opportunities you will have to work on the next day, and the approach you will take to build trust.

Step 4 – Involve Others
   (Seek feedback and support)

Think about the feedback and support you might need. Identify individuals who can provide that feedback and support, and decide how you will engage them to help you.

Build a support network.

Share your plan, successes, and less successful attempts with your manager, direct reports, peers, family, and other colleagues.

Example: Identify a willing mentor, someone you can trust to support your changes. Don't be defensive when receiving feedback.

Step 5 – Monitor Using Success Criteria
   (Transfer learning into next steps)

Plan how you will monitor your success using the criteria you set for each of your changes.

Determine regular times to review your plan on your own and with your support members.

Determine how you will monitor your progress daily.

When you have met your success criteria, focus on a new change, pursue mastery, and/or teach others.

From Thought to Action

Planning is useless without action. Just five minutes a day, used wisely, can make a tremendous difference. Set triggers that alert you to take action. Use the following techniques to help you achieve your objectives and outcomes. Your mind will provide the guidance.

> ➤ Reflect on what you have learned each day, finding a way to work this into your regular routine. Review this book for your insights.
> ➤ Commit each day to work on development.

> ➤ Seek opportunities to link your action steps to things you are already doing. Try a new way of approaching something on the job, reflecting on what went well and what you would do differently the next time.

> ➤ Be proactive—focus on skills, and add a new challenge to your routine tasks.

> ➤ Take intelligent risks after you have examined your fears.

> ➤ Stretch yourself outside your safety zone and experience the discomfort of development.

> ➤ Give yourself permission to be a novice.

> ➤ Reframe the definition of failure to overcome your fear of it.

Personal Plan: Template

Changing Your Behavior and Skills (How to build trust and eliminate fear)

Use the following form to record the changes you have chosen for greater focus, specific objectives, action plan, the involvement of others you require, and your timeline for completion.

STEP 1	STEP 2	STEP 3	STEP 4
Opportunities for Change	Action Plan	Involvement of Others	Timeline
1) Objectives			
2) Objectives			
3) Objectives			

Courageous Conversations

A useful way to sustain change is to ask your manager and direct reports how you are doing. It takes courage to ask and then receive the feedback and act upon it. I suggest incorporating this idea into your personal plan for change.

	With Managers	With Direct Reports
Before Session	Plan length, location, and what to share. Schedule session. Prepare introductory statement.	Plan length, location, and what to share. Schedule session. Prepare introductory statement.
During Session	State purpose; thank them. Clarify roles. Share reactions to your feedback. Ask clarifying questions. Ask for their perspective on the key success factors for your changes.	State purpose; thank them. Emphasize anonymity. Share at least one important perception learned. Share development objectives and success criteria and ask for input.

	With Managers	With Direct Reports
	Discuss development objectives. Ask for input. Discuss potential obstacles. Identify time frames for follow-up meetings.	Share why you chose the changes you did and how they relate to improved results on business objectives. Listen, and paraphrase feedback. Specify the most useful type of ongoing feedback they could provide, as well as how and when you can best hear it. Discuss when and how you will ask for specific feedback and check in on your progress.
After Session	Ask manager to observe performance and provide feedback.	Take immediate action on feedback. Actively seek ongoing input.

"The traditional formula for organizational success—good people, good values, and good

strategy—is woefully inadequate to meet today's challenges. Although the traditional formula remains a necessary foundation for success, leaders who play a big-stakes game know they need to go beyond the formula. They understand that a complex and changing environment requires a new way of thinking and behaving."
(Malandro, 2009)

Summary of Chapter 3

This chapter presented tools for identifying fear in a workpace, including examples of meetings in which the fear of feeling *rejected or inadequate* was the underlying factor in decisions and behaviors. The chapter also provided instructions for creating a personal action plan for moving from a place of fear to trust, in both personal and workplace situations. It offered specific communication strategies for interacting with employees and managers in ways that promote a work environment based on trust. Chapter 3 provided simple, easy-to-use tools for changing your behavior and skills to build trust and eliminate fear.

Your Reflections About Chapter 3

_____

_____

_____

_____

_____

_____

_____

_____

_____

_____

_____

_____

_____

Closing Thoughts

I would like to celebrate and acknowledge the executives, managers, employees, colleagues, friends, family, and all those who are committed to managing, reducing, and eliminating fear in the workplace. It takes courage!

With the awareness, the tools, and an action plan, you can make a difference not only in your own life, but also in the lives of those you touch each day in your organization.

Take the risk to create a new vision,
a workplace free of fear,
where relationships are built on a
foundation of trust.

Learning

Let me learn from the Mastery of others.

Let me transcend my own experience and find
new pathways to knowledge.

Let me accept different perspectives, try new
methods, and contemplate new visions.

May I always walk on the path toward Mastery,
approaching each pebble, each obstacle,
each crevice
as an opportunity to increase my capacity and
to deepen my wisdom.

May I take what I learn from mastering
each challenge and strengthen my approach
to the next.

May I always guide others whom I meet on
the learning path, lovingly and gently,
sharing wisdom.

Learning is our shared journey in love.

—*Marie Knapp*

Thomas J. Yagos Biography

Tom Yagos is the founder of Yagos & Associates, a consulting practice that focuses on building relationships in the workplace to achieve organizational effectiveness. Tom teaches employees to understand the concept of fear and recognize the symptoms and patterns of fear-based behavior, as well as how to use tools to manage and eliminate fear in both their personal and professional lives.

A coach, facilitator, speaker, writer, and teacher, Tom has 35 years of senior management experience. His visionary thinking helps organizations inspire their workforce to meet the challenges and demands of today's rapidly changing business world.

Tom is an affiliate faculty at Regis University's School of Management, where he teaches leadership development and strategy in the working-adult MBA program. His program enlightens and inspires participants to change their lives so they experience greater joy and fulfillment.

Tom's lifelong vision is to transform the workplace to be free of fear so relationships can be experienced with acceptance, enjoyment, and trust. This, he believes, is the final frontier for human engagement and organizational effectiveness.

A CD by Tom Yagos that provides an overview of the concepts for continued learning is available through his website.

For inquires, contact Tom at:

303-888-0147
Tom@YagosAssociates.com
www.YagosAssociates.com

References

Covey, Stephen M.R. *The Speed of Trust: The One Thing That Changes Everything.* New York, NY: Simon & Schuster Free Press, 2006.

Giltow, H.S. and Giltow, S.J. *The Deming Guide to Quality and Competitive Position.* New York, NY: Prentice Hall, 1987.

Hamel, Gary. "Moon Shots for Management," Harvard Business Review, Feb. 2009 (pp. 91-98).

Hurley, R. "Managing The Decision to Trust," Harvard Business Review, 2006 (p. 55).

Malandro, Loretta. *How To Overcome Behavioral Blind Spots AND Transform Your Organization.* New York, NY: McGraw-Hill, 2009.

Renia, D.S. and Renia, M.L. *Trust & Betrayal in the Workplace: Building Effective Relationships in Your Organization.* San Francisco, CA; Berrett-Koehler Publishers, 1999.

Roselle, Bruce. *Fearless Leadership: Conquering Your Fears and the Lies That Drive Them.* Minneapolis, MN: Leader Press, 2006.

Ryan, K.D. and Oestreich, D.K. *Driving Fear Out of the Workplace Creating the High-Trust, High-Performance Organization.* San Francisco, CA: Jossey-Bass, 1998 (2nd Edition).

Shaw, Robert B. *Trust in the Balance: Building Successful Organizations on Results, Integrity and Concern.* San Francisco, CA: Jossey-Bass, 1997.

Schweyer Allen. "Managing the Decision to Trust," Human Capital Institute, Jul. 2009.

Walton, Mary. *Deming Management at Work.* New York, NY: G.P. Putman's Sons, 1990 (p. 18).

Praise for *Fearless Leadership*

"Whatever situational, short-term results are perceived to be gained by fear in the workplace, they are more than outweighed by the long-term negative on people, processes, culture, and results. Organizations and leaders should focus on creating positive energy in all interactions with others."

— David B. Perez

President & CEO, Caridian BCT Inc. & Terumo Transfusion

"Fear in the workplace reduces employees' motivation and ability to achieve their full potential. It can cause highly engaged and productive employees to leave due to environmental stress. Even if fear is only perceived, it has an unfavorable impact on the organization's culture and financial outcomes."

— Margaret Turner

Sr. Consultant, Leadership Succession Management, Kaiser Permanente Colorado

"Driving fear out of the workplace was #8 in W. Edward Deming's list of 14 principles for improving quality and transforming the workplace, influencing such critical areas as problem-solving and collaborative team building. *Fearless Leadership* provides practical guidelines in the spirit of Deming's principles, describing a process whereby executive leadership can transform their own organization. This book deserves shelf space with the works of Deming, Crosby, and Gerand."

— Dan Guenther

Author, Educator, and Fortune 500 Change Agent

"Fear in the workplace kills: It kills employee engagement, morale, enthusiasm, and initiative. This powerful book is sorely needed at this critical time so we can conquer the fear that saps our collective energy."

— Elaine Swope, SPHR, PhD

Corporate HR Director, EI

"*Fearless Leadership* provides a simple-yet-effective framework for leaders to change behaviors. The book contains a valuable process to improve employee engagement and build a culture of trust. "

— Kevin Cory

Director, People & Culture, Vestas Blades America

"Building workplace relationships grounded in trust is essential in building high-performance organizations. Too often organizations unknowingly ground these relationships in fear. This timely book not only helps organizations to address this issue, but also provides them with the tools to make changes."

— Peter Bemski, PhD

Chair, Master of Science in Organization Leadership, Regis University

"In this important new book, Tom Yagos creates a vision of what organizational life is like in a culture of trust, and gives readers time-tested formulas for managing, reducing, and eliminating fear in the workplace. Filled with practical examples, case studies, and lessons learned, Yagos' new book shows us how the process of releasing fear, asking for peace of mind, and changing one's thought process can be used to improve personal and professional relationships. A must-read for leaders and managers who want to increase employee engagement, *Fearless Leadership* teaches powerful lessons on how to build a high-performing organization."

— Mark Bodnarczuk
Author, *Making Invisible Bureaucracy Visible*